A One Week Off Unit Study on...

HORSES

Dr. Sarah C. Julicher, DVM

Castle Heights Press, Inc

5649 Temerity Way
Bulverde, TX 78163
1-830-438-2496

ISBN 1-888717-13-0   One Week Off Series
ISBN 1-888717-14-9 Horses

Table of Contents

Topic	Page
Introduction	4
Schedule for studying <u>Horses</u>	5
Monday - planning day	6
Addresses for free info	7
Planning your field trip	8
Schedule	9
Tuesday - research	10
Who has designed the horse?	11
History of Horses and Riding	12
Conformation of a Horse	14
Parts of a Horse	15
Tack	17
Safety	20
Riding	21
"Age of A Horse"	24
Further Study	25
Wednesday - activity / study day	26
Activities	26
Essay	27
Essay outline	28
Vocabulary	29
Drawing horses	30
Drawing bits	31
What is your horsepower?	32
Book list	33
Book Report	35
Thursday - Field trip	36
Trip checklist	36
Field trip questions	37
Friday - Notebook	39
The Notebook	39
Resources	40
Internet Resources	42

Introduction

The One-Week-Off series is designed to be a free-wheeling unit study with a bit of structure. The One-Week-Off units are made for varying age levels. Several different activities are included in each area so the student/teacher can choose which ones are suitable given different ability levels and materials available. You have several choices of style of study:

One Week Off Method: Each unit may be done in a week as a way of taking a break from your normal class schedule or a longer study can be done if the student has greater interest. When doing the unit study as a One-Week-Off study, at the end of the week, the student(s) and teacher will have learned a great deal in the interest area chosen, and the student will have produced a notebook of his/her findings to be graded.

Longer Unit Study Method: When more time to study horses is desired, you have plenty of options of activities, readings, and investigations included in this volume. Simply take as much time as needed to study horses. Be sure to keep records of your researches, especially if you are in high school. In this way your can establish credit in several different areas for your transcript.

Field Trips to Library / Stable: A trip to a local university or community library is included in the week's activities for research on the subject. From knowledge gained at the library, the inquisitive student can formulate questions to be asked on the field trip later in the week. Suggestions for field trips are included in these units, but depending on where you live, you may be able to come up with some other informative and fun places to visit. Planning for the field trip is done on the first day of the week or before if advance notice is required for the trip. The field trip is to be the culmination of the week, where the student takes pictures and has his/her questions answered, all to be included in the final notebook.

Schedules: The schedule on the following page will aid in planning your week off. You will invariably learn much about the subject area no matter what schedule you use, but scheduling will help you plan for your research. Whatever scheduling method you use, studying horses will be fun, so enjoy!

Important Notes

This unit study is designed so that students of many different abilities will find some interesting topics to pursue or activities to do. There are activities for the new rider as well as activities for more experienced riders.

The unit study may be done by students who want less structure than the One-Week-Off format uses. This is easily done by just skipping the schedule on page five and using your own schedule.

Schedule For One Week Off Format

Monday

Planning Day

Make phone calls to schedule field trip

Study activities and questions

Decide which ones you will do

Make list of topics for library

Start research on the internet

Write letters to send off for free items. Be sure to copy them for your notebook before you send them.

Tuesday

Research Day

Trip to library
1. Books to read
2. Info for research

Draw pictures

Read books

Copy letters written Monday to put in notebook

Answer questions from chosen topic areas listed in Tuesday section

Write essays

Wednesday

Study/Activity Day

Polish and rewrite essays

Do chosen activities: book report, model horse, etc.

Return trip to library if necessary

Write down questions for field trip

Read books

Thursday

Field Trip Day

Go on trip

Ask questions

Write down the answers

Take pictures on trip

Develop photos

Write thank you note to guide

Friday

Notebook Day

Develop/pick up photos

Return library books

Mail thank you note (copy it first)

Complete any unfinished activities

Put together notebook

The first day is set aside for organizing the week, as you can see on the schedule. You should decide which activities you will be doing and make sure you have the required materials to do the activities. Consider buying clay at your local hobby store, going through your own personal library to determine what references and materials you already have, and obtaining directions to the nearest university library and riding academy.

You will need to develop a list of topics to research at the library. To do this, you must read the sections for the rest of the week to get an idea of what you wish to study.

There are several places the student can write to for free information in the field of horses and riding. Monday is the day for the student to compose letters to be sent to these places. A copy of the letters can be made when you go to the library, and the copies will be included for grading in the notebook to be compiled on Friday.

Castle Heights Press, Inc.

Addresses for Free Info

1. Dover Saddlery
   Box 5837
   Holliston, MA 01746
   Catalog (English)

2. Jockey Club (Thoroughbred)
   300 Park Ave.
   New York, NY 10022
   Brochure

3. American Warmblood Registry
   P.O. Box 15167
   Tallahasee, FL
   32317-5167
   Brochure

4. The American Saddlebred Horse Association
   Dept. HI
   4093 Iron Works Pike
   Lexington, KY 40511
   Brochure

5. Peruvian Paso Promotions
   Box 4851 - HR
   Chico, CA 95927
   Brochure

6. U. S. Trotting Association
   750 Michigan Ave.
   Columbus, OH 43215
   Brochure

7. The International Arabian Horse Association
   10805 East Bethany Drvie
   Aurora, CO 80014

8. Arab Horse World Quarterly / Online
   1316 Tamson Drive Suite 101
   Cambria, CA 93428
   www.ahwmagazine.com
   Ask about the essay contest for under 14 year olds.

98. American Horse Shows Association
   527 Madison Ave.
   New York, NY   10022
   Brochure

10. State Line Tack Inc.
   Rt. 121
   P.O. Box 1217
   Plaistow, NH 03865-1217
   Catalog (Western and English)

11. American Quarter Horse Association
   P.O. Box 200
   Amarillo, TX 79168
   Ask for "bro 13" for an assortment of
   various brochures. Ask for specific titles for
   free posters, charts, and other good stuff.

12. 4-H
   Check with your local county agricultral extension agent:
   For example, in Tennessee:
   4-H -Tennessee
   Extension Animal Science- beef, sheep, horse
      The University of Tennessee
      Institute of Agriculture
      P.O. Box 1071
      Knoxville, TN 37901-1071
      865-974-7294
   Even if out of state, you can order materials.

13. American Pony Club
   extension agent for information about
   the local 4-H Club. Try the Yellow Pages.
   ponyclub.org
      4041 Iron Wroks Parkway
      Lexoington, KY 40511
      859-254-7669

14. Breyers Model Horses

15. Morgan Horse Association
   www.morganhorse.com
      122 Bostwick
      P.O. Box 960
      Shelburne, VT 05482

16. American Mule Association
      P.O. Box 6
      Clovis, CA 93613-0006

17. American Donkey and Mule Association
      2901 N. Elm Street
      Denton, TX 16201
      940-382-6845
   www.admsdonkeyandmule.com

18. Canadian Donkey and Mule Association
      RR 2, Site 1, Box 15
      Rocky Mountain House
      Alberta, Canada
      TOM 1TO
      403-845-5308

Castle Heights Press, Inc.

Plan Your Field Trip

You will need to schedule your field trip today as well. According to this schedule, the planned time for your field trip is Thursday, but if you cannot arrange it then, you can plan your schedule accordingly.

To begin your study of horses, the best thing to do is to go to a local riding academy and take an orientation lesson. The cost will usually be $20 - $30 and will have great educational value.

In an average beginning lesson, you will learn several things (Note: styles of instruction vary, so don't worry if your instructor teaches in a different order or uses a slower progression.):
1. Basic grooming
2. Tacking up and untacking
3. Mounting and dismounting
4. Basic gaits and diagonals
5. Leading a horse

During your call to the riding academy, you should ask a few questions such as: "Do they supply helmets for the beginning class?" and "What do you teach in a first lesson?" Note: To build self confidence and gain experience, an older student should make this call herself.

Plan to wear jeans and sturdy shoes (boots if you have them).

The End of the Planning Day

When you have outlined and arranged the rest of your unit study, you are through with your planning day. Each student should have his or her course of action laid out: what activities to focus on, in which areas to develop questions for the field trip, and what to research at the library tomorrow.

The planning forms on the following pages will aid you in laying out your course plan.

Schedule Form

General Topic	Resources
Research questions	
	Websites
Activity	**Materials**

Castle Heights Press, Inc.

Tuesday- research

Tuesday is library day. On this day the student will research interesting topics on horses and riding.

The questions here are to guide the student in researching horses. These are fundamental to the topic and should lead students into more detailed areas. Additional topics are included so you can develop your own questions. Any of these questions can be modified or researched in lesser detail depending on the ability level of the student. The starred questions are more advanced and will require more time and thought to answer.

> You probably will not have time to cover all of these sections much less all the questions unless you are plannig to spend more than a week studying horses and riding.

You should complete the unstarred, basic questions in each section before proceeding to the more advanced questions. This way you will gain more from your research. At the library, look for the books listed in the references section of the appendix for your research. If there are questions you can not find answers for or do not understand, call the local riding academy and talk to one of the instructors on staff. They love to talk horses.

The underlined words are key words to be looked up in an encyclopedia and to aid in finding more information on the topic.

The activities outlined in this section can either be done at the end of the library trip or on Wednesday, but they are listed here as continuations of the topics. In Wednesday's section, there are coordinated pages to accompany the activities listed here.

> *Be sure to keep track of the books you use in your research, as you will need the title, author, publisher, and publication date to include in your notebook's bibliography section.*

Castle Heights Press, Inc.

Who has Designed the Horse?

Do you give the horse his strength or clothe his neck with a flowing mane?

Do you make him leap like a locust, striking terror with his proud snorting?

He paws fiercely, rejoicing in his strength, and charges into the fray.

He laughs at fear, afriad of nothing; he does not shy away from the sword.

The quiver rattles against his side, along with the flashing spear and lance.

In frenzied excitment he eats up the ground; he cannot stand still when the trumpet sounds.

At the blast of the trumpet he snorts 'Aha!'

He catches the scent of battle from afar, the shout of commanders and the battle cry.

Job 39:19-25

Graphic border with chariot

Castle Heights Press, Inc.

History of Horses and Riding

Riding horses was one of the earliest modes of transportation. Horses are stronger and faster than humans and so it is easy to see why people decided to use horses for transportation of people and possessions. The tools, or tack, used while riding have changed through the years and the history of those changes influenced the history of civilization.

Questions

1. What are some different ways people have used horses in their civilizations?

2. Which people were the first to keep records of their horses' ancestry or breeding? Which horse was it?

*3. Think of three different methods you would use to catch wild horses. What would you need to do it and how hard would it be? Do you need more people. Draw a diagram showing the method you would prefer.

4. The bridle is used to control the horse's head. How does the bridle help the rider? *Hint: what does the rider do with the bridle? When was the bridle first used?*

5. Stirrups were used by the Mongolians in their conquests. How did this help them fight? How did this help them fight against their enemies who did not have stirrups?

6. Did the Romans have stirrups during their conquests?

7. Renaissance riding is an interesting study. One resource is <u>The Development of Modern Riding</u> by Vladimir S. Lattuer published by the Howell House Publishing, 1991.

Castle Heights Press, Inc.

History of Horses and Riding (continued)

8. Give three reasons why the army of Genghis Khan was nearly invincible. Their horses were a significant advantage to them as they raided the plains. What ways did they use their horses to give them greater military advantages? Hints: stirrups, chain of command, control, and comunications, pony express type of communication with the rest of the empire.

9. Why did the Knights of the Middle Ages armor their war horses? How did this impact the size and strength of the horses they choose to fight with? Note: to answer this question, you will need to find out how the knights fought. What kind of armor did they use and how did it affect their mobility on the horse and on the ground?

10. How did the horse affect the Conquest of Mexico? The natives had never seen horses before and this gave Montezuma a great advantage militarily. What was the psychology of war used by the Spaniards?

11. Where did the Native Americans get their horses? What did they first use horses for? What specific tribes first caught on to the idea of riding horses? What types of tack did they use and what did they make it out of?

12. The Western saddle was developed in the expansion of the American West. What are some of its features and how were they used? Why was the Spanish saddle used in this development instead of the English saddle?

Activity #1: Research and make a report on history of your favorite breed. Include the names and locations of any famous sires and dams. Include a paragraph on the achievements of this breed.

Activity #2: Make a map showing the Mongolian Expansion, the Roman conquests of Europe, or the Mohammedan conquests

Activity #3. Make a timeline showing one or more of: the development of riding tack, the domestication of the horse, the development of modern breeds of horse, or the development of modern riding styles.

Castle Heights Press, Inc.

Conformation of a Horse

1. Why can you tell the age of a horse by its teeth? By what characteristics can you tell the age? Hint: You can only tell the age of a horse accurately by the teeth up to about eight.

*2. What is the effect of having long cannon bones as opposed to short cannons?

3. Why is the horse fuzzy in the wintertime?

4. Why are draft horses' hooves splayed out?

5. Why we do shoe horses?

*6. Compare the main differences between short-coupled and long-coupled horses. Note: The idea is to learn about differences in the structure of the horse and how a rider must use trade-offs when choosing a horse. Coupling: Refers to the length between the last rib and the point of the hip (or lumbar region of the horse's spine). Hint: Look at a diagram of the skeleton of a horse. What is different about this area from other areas of the horse's spine. Think in terms of where the rider's weight is on the horse's back.

	Short-coupled horse	Long-coupled horse
Strength		
Ride comfort		
Flexibility		
Related conformational differences such as cannon length		
Specific use advantages of each		

7. Read the story of The Trojan Horse. How did the Greeks use the horse to destroy the city?

8. Explain the proverb "Don't look a gift horse in the mouth."

Activity #4: Shown in the drawing on the next page are the parts of a typical horse. Sketch or trace different breeds of horses found in your library books such as: Arabian, Shire, Thoroughbred, Trakehner, Quarter Horse, Shetland pony. On some of your drawings, label the parts of the horse.

Castle Heights Press, Inc.

Parts of A Horse

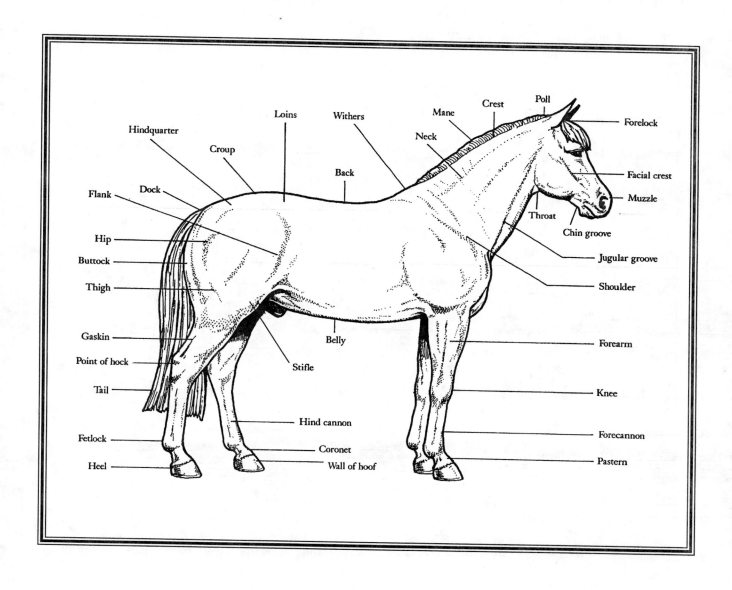

Loins · Withers · Mane · Crest · Poll · Forelock · Hindquarter · Neck · Croup · Back · Flank · Dock · Facial crest · Muzzle · Hip · Throat · Chin groove · Buttock · Jugular groove · Thigh · Shoulder · Gaskin · Belly · Forearm · Point of hock · Stifle · Tail · Knee · Hind cannon · Fetlock · Forecannon · Coronet · Heel · Wall of hoof · Pastern

Castle Heights Press, Inc.

Conformation of a Horse (continued)

*9. How often in a year does a horse shed out its coat?

*10. The angles in a horse's leg are important for the strength, flexibility, shock absorption, and power of the animal. Draw a horse leg and identify the angles in the joints. Compare to a photograph of a horse. Measure the angles of that horse. Which joints should have angles and which should not? What is the commonly accepted correct angle for the pastern?

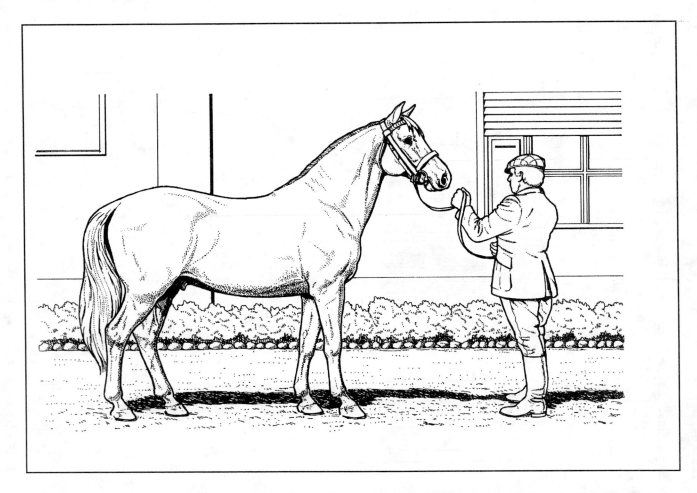

Activity #5: Are the eyes of a horse monocular, binocular, or both? Draw a picture showing the range of vision of the horse from the top.

Activity #6: Do all four hooves of the horse leave the ground at the same time at the gallop? Check out the moving horsephotos on this website:

    Legacy of the Horse:
              www.imh.org/imh/kyhplb.html

        Castle Heights Press, Inc.

Tack

DOUBLE BRIDLE

Tack is a general term for all equipment pertaining to a horse. The basic tack used for riding includes saddles, bridles, bits, and girths.

In the United States, there are two major divisions of riding styles: Western and English. The Western style developed from the practical usage of herding cattle and the English from the more formalized sports of fox hunting and racing in England.

1. List some of the things you would need to put on the horse in order to ride.

_____

_____

_____

_____

_____

_____

2. On a Western show saddle there is lots of silver. Why is this not the case on an English show saddle?

*3. What did the Native Americans in your area use to ride?

4. What do you need a bit for? Where does it go?

5. What is a horn on a Western saddle and how is it used?

6. Why do some people braid the mane and tail?

7. What is a martingale and how is it used?

8. Why is it necessary to have the girth tight?

9. What are the average prices of good equipment? Call several suppliers (or order their catalogs) and record their prices. Use the chart below:

Tack Item	Supplier/price	Supplier/price	Supplier/price	Supplier/price
saddle:				
bridle:				
girth:				

Castle Heights Press, Inc.

Tack

Activity #7: Identify the uses of various pieces of tack.

Tack Item	Comfort/ Support	Control	Safety/Protection	Communication
Saddle				
Bridle				
Crop				
Girth				
Reins				
Bit				
German Martingale				
Stirrup				
Saddle pad				
Snaffle Bit				
Spurs				
Halter				
Lunge Line				
Breastplate				
Hackmore				
Splint Boots				
Horse Blanket				
Fly Mask				
Saddle Horn				
Shoes				
Pelham Bit				
Caveson				
Hobbles				

Castle Heights Press, Inc.

Tack (continued)

BOSAL

10. What is a halter used for?

Activity #8: Draw one Westen bit and one English bit.

Activity #9: Label each bit and state the primary mode of action on the horse's head. (Hint: Where is the most pressure exerted?)

Castle Heights Press, Inc.   19

Safety

Safety around horses is essential to the the knowledge of each and every horseperson. Basic safety must be known no matter if you are just a weekend rider or you are going to spend your life with horses. **Note: Be sure to answer all of this section before you go on your field trip.**

1. Why should you wear hard-toed boots when around horses?

2. On an English saddle, why do you always run up the stirrup irons when not in use?

3. Why would you put a red ribbon in a horse's tail?

4. Why should you <u>always</u> wear a safety helmet while riding?

5. When turning the horse from the ground, should you turn toward the horse or away from the horse? Why?

6. Why do you never wrap the lead rope or reins around your wrist?

7. Why should you never run or shout around a horse?

8. How should a treat be given to a horse safely?

9. When grooming and saddling a horse, how should you change sides or go around the horse safely? Demonstrate to a parent or sibling using a pair of chairs or a long table as your horse. Don't forget to use a lead rope or cross ties to restrain your 'horse'.

　　　　Castle Heights Press, Inc.

Riding

1. Why do you keep your heels down?

*2. Although at first looked down upon during its early devel‹ ment, the Forward Seat style of riding was a revolution in the world of equitation (invented by Capt. Federico Caprilli). Hur seat riding and the modern racing seat are the most common examples seen today. How does the forward seat affect the horse and rider?

For resources:

1. The Art of Riding by Lt Col. M.F. McTaggart, D.S.O., Arc Books, Inc. New York, 1963. Originally published in 1930, as a series of articles in the Morning Post..

2. Riding forward, or Modern Horsemanship for Beginners by Vladimir s. Littauer, Howell Books, New York, 1962.

3. Form Over Fences by Jane M. Dillon, D. Van Nostrand Inc., New York, 1961.

3. What is posting? Why would you post? Is it possible to post a trot without stirrups?

4. What is the Around the World exercise?

5. Demonstrate how you hold the reins.

In Western?

In English?

*6. How do you tell the proper diagonal for a posting trot?

*7. How do you tell the proper lead for a canter?

8. Is there an advantage in wearing breeches or chaps while riding? If so, what is it?

Castle Heights Press, Inc.

9. Complete this chart on basic riding gaits:

Characteristic	Walk	Trot/Jog	Canter/Lope	Gallop
Speed				
Position of rider				
Post /no post?				
Hoof pattern				
Rhythm				

10. What are some of the differences between dressage and reining?

Characteristic	Dressage	Reining
Position of rider		
Control of horse(aids)?		
Tack?		
Overall Style?		
Frame of horse?		
Judging points		

Castle Heights Press, Inc.

Riding (continued)

11. Name the natural aids.

12. Here is a list of artificial aids. Tell why are they used.

Artificial aid	Method used
Crop	
Spurs	
Martingale	
Lunge Whip	
Side Reins	
Chambon	
Flash Nose band	
Shock Collar	

13. What are the differences between a direct rein and a neck rein?

14. What is a pulley rein?

*15. Artificial gaits or man-made gaits are unnatural to the horse. What are the names of three of these gaits? When are they used and by what breeds?

Activity #7: Make a list of Western and English riding activities you can do for fun.

———————————————   ———————————————

———————————————   ———————————————

———————————————   ———————————————

Activity #8: Do the horsepower problems on page 36.

Castle Heights Press, Inc.

The Age of a Horse

To tell the age of any horse,
 Inspect the lower jaw of course;
The six front teeth the tale will tell,
And every doubt and fear dispel.

Two middle nippers you behold,
Before the colt is two years old;
Before eight weeks, two more will come.
Eight months the corners cut the gum.

The outside grooves will disapear
From middle two in just one year;
In two years from the second pair-
In three years the "corners" too are bare.

At two the middle "nippers" drop;
At three the second pair can't stop;
When four years old the third pair goes,
At five a full new set he shows.

The deep black spots will pass from view
At six years, from the middle two;
The second pair at seven years,
At eight the spot each corner clears.

From middle "nippers" upper jaw,
At nine the black spots will withdraw;
The second pair at ten are bright,
Eleven finds the corners light.

As time goes on the horsemen know
The oval teeth three-sided grow;
They longer get, project before,
Till twenty-when we know no more.

Anonymous

 Castle Heights Press, Inc.

Further Study

In addition to the topics detailed above, you may want to delve into other areas after you have covered the basics (the unstarred questions). To give you some ideas, here are some topics to consider:

- Competition
- Jumping
- Dressage
- Team roping
- Gymkhana
- Trail riding
- Eventing
- 4-H
- Pony club
- Hunting

Castle Heights Press, Inc.

Wednesday- activities/study

Activities

On Wednesday, the day before your field trip, you should apply what you learned at the library in the form of activities. As you encountered these activities while doing the research and questioning of the previous section, you will have seen a few that you wanted to do. You may do as many activities as you have the time and interest. In this section are forms and further information to help you do the activities you have chosen.

Essay

Today you should correct your essay written yesterday and produce a final copy to include in your compiled notebook which you will put together on Friday.

Field Trip Questions

A very important item to complete today is your list of questions to ask on your field trip tomorrow. There are suggestions in this section for questions to ask a horseperson should you be able to visit a riding academy. Use your newfound knowledge to put together as many questions as possible. You should write these on notebook paper or type them, with space left between the questions so you can write the answers as you acquire them. This will also go into your final notebook.

  Castle Heights Press, Inc.

Essay

At the end of your day at the library, it will be time to write an essay on what you have learned. This essay should be timed, as an exercise in writing quickly and concisely in an organized manner. For high school students used to writing essays, the time limit should be 20-30 minutes. Younger students can be allowed more, say about 35-45 minutes. A good essay consists of an introduction, outlining the topic and main points of the essay; a main body, usually one paragraph for each main point; and a conclusion; summing up the arguments of the essay. The teacher should choose one of the previous topics, then announce the topic at the beginning of the timed period.

Some topics you might choose are:

When is a training method inhumane?
Why should you use a helmet while riding?
Are stirrups useful?
What are some advantages to a round pen?
Why I should be allowed to own a horse

Note: As a horse must be collected in order to perform a flying lead change, so you must collect your thoughts in order to write an essay. This page is designed to help you in doing just that. Below is a sample essay outline. Follow this general format in writing your own outline and essay.

Essay Outline

Title _____

I. Introduction: Thesis showing three main points

II. First main point
    A. Subheading -supports first main point
        1. Detail -supports subheading A

        2. Detail -supports subheading A

    B. Subheading -supports first main point
        1. Detail -supports subheading B

        2. Detail -supports subheading B

III. Second main point
    A. Subheading -supports second main point
        1. Detail -supports subheading A

        2. Detail -supports subheading A

    B. Subheading -supports second main point
        1. Detail -supports subheading B

        2. Detail -supports subheading B

IV. Third main point
    A. Subheading -supports third main point
        1. Detail -supports subheading A

        2. Detail -supports subheading A

    B. Subheading -supports third main point
        1. Detail -supports subheading B

        2. Detail -supports subheading B

V. Conclusion: Restatement of thesis and main points

 Castle Heights Press, Inc.

Vocabulary

Parts of a Horse

Cannon
Chestnut
Coronary Band
Crest
Croup
Dock
Fetlock
Flank
Forelock
Frog
Gaskin
Girth
Heel
Hock
Hoof
Loin
Pastern
Poll
Stifle
Tail
Throatlatch
Wither

General

Aids
Appointments
Bearing Rein
Billet Strap
Bit
Bitting
Blanket
Boots
Breastplate
Bridle
Cantle
Cinch
Collection
Colt
Cooler
Crop
Curb
Curry comb
Dandy brush
Dam
Extension
Filly
Foal
Gelding
Girth
Groom
Hack
Hackamore
Halter
Harness
Helmet
Hoof pick
Lead rope
Lunge line
Mare
Martingale
Pelham
Pommel
Quirt
Reins
Saddle
Saddle horn
Saddlepad
Sire
Snaffle
Stallion
Stirrup

Gaits

Walk
Trot
Jog
Pace
Canter
Lope
Hand Gallop
Gallop
Racing Gallop

Running Walk
Slow Gait
Rack
Tolt
Paso
Fox Trot
Amble
Skeid

Castle Heights Press, Inc.

Name: _____

Date: _____

Breed: _____

Activity #3: Horse Drawing

Castle Heights Press, Inc.

Name: _____

Date: _____

Type of Bit: _____

Name: _____

Date: _____

Type of Bit: _____

What is Your Horsepower?

(Students with heart problems should not attempt this experiment)

Materials

Stopwatch
Ruler or
Measuring tape

Power is the tine/rate of doing work. James Watt determined that the aveage horse could lift a 550 pound weight one foot in one second or 550 ft/lb per sec. This is the standard horsepower measurement. You can measure your own horsepower by the following technique.

1. Record your weight in the table.

2. Measure the height of a flight of stairs in feet. this is done by measuring one stair and multiplying the height by the number of stairs.

3. Run up the stairs as fast as you can and record your time in seconds. Repeat 3 times.

4. Multiply your weight times the height of the stairs to find the amount of work done.

5. Divide the work done by the time in seconds to find the amount of work done in one second.

6. Now determine your horsepower by using the formula

$$H.P. = \frac{ft./lb. \ per \ sec.}{550}$$

	Your weight in pounds	Total height climbed (number of steps X the height of one step)	Time in seconds to go upstairs	Total work done (weight X height of stairs）	Work for each second = foot-lbs per second)	H.P. = $\frac{ft./lb. \ per \ sec.}{550}$
Trial 1						
Trial 2						
Trial 3						

Castle Heights Press, Inc.

Book List

Title: _____

Author: _____

Subject: _____

Publisher: _____

Title: _____

Author: _____

Subject: _____

Publisher: _____

Title: _____

Author: _____

Subject: _____

Publisher: _____

Title: _____

Author: _____

Subject: _____

Publisher: _____

Title: _____

Author: _____

Subject: _____

Publisher: _____

Title: _____

Author: _____

Subject: _____

Publisher: _____

Title: _____

Author: _____

Subject: _____

Publisher: _____

Book List (continued)

Title: _____

Author: _____

Subject: _____

Publisher: _____

Title: _____

Author: _____

Subject: _____

Publisher: _____

Title: _____

Author: _____

Subject: _____

Publisher: _____

Title: _____

Author: _____

Subject: _____

Publisher: _____

Title: _____

Author: _____

Subject: _____

Publisher: _____

Title: _____

Author: _____

Subject: _____

Publisher: _____

Title: _____

Author: _____

Subject: _____

Publisher: _____

Castle Heights Press, Inc.

Title:_____

Author:_____

Publisher and Copyright date:_____

1. Who is this book written about?

2. In what aspect of riding was this person involved? What important principles did they discover, if any?

3. Was there an event in this person's childhood which sparked an interest in horses? What was it?

4. What type of horsemanship education did this person receive?

5. What godly character qualities did this person have? i.e. diligence, perserverance, etc.

6. Did this person benefit the field of equitation or mankind as a whole? How?

7. What things did this person do with his/her life beyond horse-related activities ?

Thursday- field trip

Trip Checklist:

1. **Clothing:** Wear proper gear for riding. Sturdy shoes, comfortable jeans, helmet (probably provided free by the academy).

2. **Questions:** No matter where you go on your field trip, the important thing is to get your questions answered. Take your list of questions on a clipboard or in a notebook so you can write down the answers as you get them.

3. **Camera and film:** Take lots of pictures for documentation. If you are at a riding academy, get pictures of the different horses you see. At the end of the day, take your pictures to be developed in an hour or overnight, so you will have them to put in your notebook on Friday.

4. **Thank you note:** When you get back, write a thank you note for your instructor. You can get the instructor's name and address while you are at the riding academy. Make sure you photocopy this letter for your notebook before you send it.

Castle Heights Press, Inc.

Field Trip Questions

It has already been mentioned many times in this book that you need to put together a list of questions to ask on your field trip. Assuming you can get to a riding academy to talk to an instructor, the following questions are some that you could ask him or her. Look at the questions and perhaps they will help to come up with some of your own. Also if you did not find the answers to some of your research question, you may ask the riding instructor.

1. What is the best part of riding?

_____

_____

_____

_____

2. When did you first ride? How old were you?

_____

_____

_____

_____

3. What is your favorite style of riding and why?

_____

_____

_____

4. Which style of riding is easiest to learn?

_____

_____

_____

5. Why do I have to wear a helmet?

_____

_____

_____

6. In your experience, what is the hardest thing to learn as a riding student? What is the easiest? Most dangerous?

_____

_____

7. How long does it take a mare to have a foal?

_____

_____

_____

8. How much does a horse cost?

_____

_____

_____

9. What would you tell a person who is interested in acquiring a horse to do or aviod?

_____

_____

_____

_____

10. _____

_____

_____

_____

_____

11. _____

_____

_____

_____

_____

12. _____

_____

_____

_____

13. _____

_____

_____

_____

_____

_____

_____

Castle Heights Press, Inc.

Friday- notebook

1. **Notebook.** Today you will conclude the week's activities as you compile a notebook of everything you have done. Your notebook can be a three-ring binder or a folder- something you can add pages to. Before you include your written things (essay, questions), make final copies of them so that your notebook is neat. This notebook can be graded if so desired. Be sure to date everything as you put it in the notebook.
2. **Pictures.** Develop your pictures if you have not already done so.
3. **Books.** Return all library books.
3. **Letters.** Mail your thank you note and your letters written on Monday if you haven't done so.

The Notebook:

☐   1. Title page (title, name, date).

☐   2. Book report.

☐   3. Essay.

☐   4. Letters written on Monday, thank-you-note to instructor.

☐   5. Field trip questions and answers.

☐   6. Any drawings you have done, all labeled.

☐   7. Photos.

☐   8. Bibliography of books used in this study.

Resources

1. All About Horses
   Margurite Henry
   Random House OP

2. Basic Horsemanship: English and Western
   Eleanor F. Prince and Gaydell M. Collier
   Doubleday, Garden City; 1974

3. Hunter Seat Equitation
   George H. Morris
   Doubleday 1990

4. Live Stock and Complete Stock Doctor: A Cyclopedia
   A. H. Barker
   H. L. Baldwin Pub. Co., Minneapolis; 1911 OP

5. The Art of Horsemanship
   Xenophon
   Translated by M. H. Morgan Ph.D.
   J. A. Allen and Co., London; 1962

6. Eyewitness Handbook of Horses
   Elwyn Hartley Edwards
   Dorling Kindersley Inc., New York: 1993

7. My Pony, My Horse
   Cherry Hill
   Storey Publishing

8. Basic Training; Backyard Dressage
   Mary Twelveponies.
   A. S. Barnes & Co, Inc., 1980
   She has several very good books such as
There are No Problem Horses,
   on training.

9. Lyons on Horses
   John Lyons
   Doubleday, 1991

10. The Horse 2nd Edition
    J. W. Evans, A. Borton, H. F. Hintz, & L.
       D. Van Vleck
    W. H. Freeman and Company. 1990.
    Illustrated encyclopedia of horses and horse care.

11. Form to Function : A Video
    American Quarter Horse Association
    Free loan reservations should be directed to:
    AQHA Video Tapes
    American Quarter Horse Association
    P.O. Box 200
    Amarillo, TX 79168

12. Imprinting   A video
    Robert Miller, DVM

13. The Usborne Book of Pony Care and Riding
    Usborne

14. Equal to the Challenge
    Jackie C. Burke
    Howell Book House, New York, 1997

15. Hints on Driving
    Capt. G. Morley Knight
    J. A. Allen & Company, London, 1884,
       1991

16. Bits
    Louis Taylor
    Melvin Powers Wilshire Book Company,
       Hollywood, CA,1966

17. Schooling for Young Riders
    John Richard Young
    Oklahoma University Press, Norman,
       OK, 1985

   Castle Heights Press, Inc.

18. <u>Training the Roman Calvalry</u>
    Ann Hyland
    Grange Books, London, 1993

19. <u>Starting Colts</u>
    Mike Kevil
    Western Horseman Inc., Colorado Springs,
        CO, 1999

20. <u>Legends</u>
    Diane C. Simmons
    Western Horseman Inc., Colorado Springs,
        CO, 1993

21. <u>The Black Loch</u>
    Patricia Leitch
    Funk and Wagnalls, New York; 1968

22. <u>The Black Stallion</u>
    Walter Farley
    Random House, 1971

23. <u>Year of the Horse</u>
    Rita Ritchie
    E. P. Dutton and Co., New York; 1965

24. <u>Come on Seabiscuit</u>
    Ralph Moody
    Houghton Mifflin Co., London; 1963

25. <u>My Friend Flicka</u>
    Mary O'Hara
    Harper and Row, New York; 1969

26. <u>Gypsy From Nowhere</u>
    Sharon Wagner
    Western Publishing Co. Inc.; 1975

27. <u>Black Beauty</u>
    Anna Sewell

28. <u>Susan & Jane Learn to Ride</u>
    Margaret Cabell Self
    Macrae Smth Company, Philadelphia,
        1965

Internet Resources

1. Best website for horses breeds:
www.ansi.okstate.edu/breeds/horses
Has videos and photos

2. About.com guide to horses:
http://horses.miningco.com/mbody.htm?PID=2807&COB=homge

3. The United States Pony club:
http://www.ponyclub.org/

4. Hannah Hazard (fun safety activities from the Pony Club)
http://www.ponyclub.org/Safety/HHintro.htm

5. 4 Horses a 4anything.com guide to horses:
http://www.4horses.com/

6. Horses! On the internet
http://wwwequinet.com/

7. Equine Info:
http://www.equineinfo.com/

8. HorseClick:
http://horseclick.com/

9. The Jockey Club:
http://jockeyclub.com/

10. State Line Tack:
http://www.statelinetack.com/

11. Valley Vet Supply:
http://www.valleyvet.com/

12. American Quarter Horse Association:
http://www.aqha.com/

13. United States Olympic Team:
http://uset.com

14. History of Man and Horses:
http://imh.org/imh/Kyhplb.html

15. Buffalo Soldiers on the Western Frontier:
http://imh.org/imh/buf/buftoc.html

16. American Academy of Equine Art:
www.AAEA.net/

17. Cave Equine Art:
www.culture.fr/Culture/arcnat/chauvet/en/gvpda

18. Institute of Ancient Equestrian Studies:
http://users.hartwick.edu/%7EIAES/index.htm

19. University of Florida Natural History Museum:
www.Flmnh.ufl.edu/natsci/vertpaleo/fhe/firstCM.htm

20. Horse Breeds of the World:
http://imh.org/imh/bio/index.html

21. Lipizzaner
www.uvi.si/eng/slovenia/lipizzaners/index.html
www.newww.com/free/lipizzaner/history.html

Castle Heights Press, Inc.

About The Author

Sarah and Cisco, a 3yr old Quarter Horse she trained in 1999

Dr. Sarah Julicher is interested in all aspects of animals. Growing up, she had experiences raising and caring for a wide variety of species, including dogs, cats, sheep, rabbits, hamsters fish, birds, and of course, horses. She owns a Thoroughbred named Beren that she has trained in dressage, cross-country, and show jumping and she enjoys taking him to horse shows. Some of Sarah's other interests include fencing, flying, amatuer radio, and writing poetry. Currently, Sarah is a veterinarian in Bulverde, Texas. Contact Sarah at: julicher@constainia.net

A Unit on Horses

This is the well-known unit study on horses by Sarah Julicher. Join the hundreds of independent learners who have used Horses as the basis for a solid academic unit.

Horses includes research questions on their history, the structure of horses, riding horses (Western and English as well as other styles), breeding, uses, tack, and the different kinds of horses. There are many resources, including internet sites and addresses to write for free information about horses. Many different activities for all ages are included.

The unit on horses may take a month or it can be used in part for a wonderful week off from your regular studies. Choose among many great activities: poems, essays, book reports, posters, and research interviews. There is a field trip planned into the unit too, complete with interview questions and things to look for at the stable.

Count the hours spent studying horses and give your student credit for doing this unit. Anywhere from 1/4 credit to a whole credit of Animal Science may be earned using this book.

There is even another unit study on horses written especially for little brothers and sisters who want to do a unit of horses, but do not yet read strongly. It is called: My First Unit Study on Horses.

1-830-438-2496

$12.95 USA
ISBN 1-888717-14-9

Castle Heights Press, Inc.

5649 Temerity Way
Bulverde, TX 78163